# Rush!

and

# Tap, Tap, Tap!

**'Rush!' and 'Tap, Tap, Tap!'**
An original concept by Katie Dale
© Katie Dale

Illustrated by Angelika Scudamore

**Published by MAVERICK ARTS PUBLISHING LTD**

Studio 3A, City Business Centre, 6 Brighton Road,

Horsham, West Sussex, RH13 5BB

© Maverick Arts Publishing Limited May 2019

+44 (0)1403 256941

A CIP catalogue record for this book is available at the British Library.

**ISBN 978-1-84886-437-5**

www.maverickbooks.co.uk

Pink

This book is rated as: Pink Band (Guided Reading)
This story is decodable at Letters and Sounds Phase 2.

# Rush!

and

# Tap, Tap, Tap!

By
Katie Dale

Illustrated by
Angelika
Scudamore

# The Letter R

*Trace the lower and upper case letter with a finger. Sound out the letter.*

*Down,
up,
around*

*Down,
up,
around,
down*

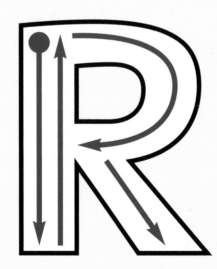

## Some words to familiarise:

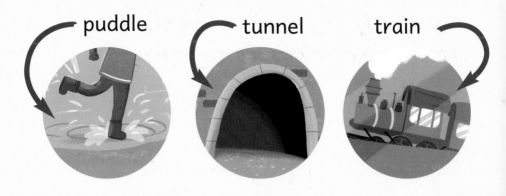

puddle     tunnel     train

## High-frequency words:

### go   to   off   the

**Tips for Reading 'Rush!'**

- Practise the words listed above before reading the story.

- If the reader struggles with any of the other words, ask them to look for sounds they know in the word.  Encourage them to sound out the words and help them read the words if necessary.

- After reading the story, ask the reader what everyone got onto in the end.

**Fun Activity**

Discuss other things that go 'puff'.

# Rush!

Run to the hill.

Puff! Puff! Puff!

# Run to the tunnel.

# Puff! Puff! Puff!

Run to the bus.

Puff! Puff! Puff!

Run to the train.

Puff! Puff! Puff!

Off we go!

# The Letter T

*Trace the lower and upper case letter with a finger. Sound out the letter.*

*Down,
lift,
cross*

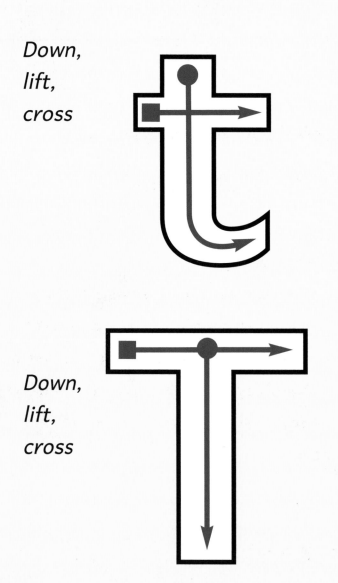

*Down,
lift,
cross*

## Some words to familiarise:

Ben    Sam    Sid

## High-frequency words:

# can   Mum   Dad

**Tips for Reading 'Tap, Tap, Tap!'**

*- Practise the words listed above before reading the story.*

*- If the reader struggles with any of the other words, ask them to look for sounds they know in the word. Encourage them to sound out the words and help them read the words if necessary.*

*- After reading the story, ask the reader why everyone was worried near the end.*

**Fun Activity**

*What noises can you make?*

# Tap, Tap, Tap!

Ben can tap.

Dad can tap.

Tap, tap, tap!

Nan can tap.

Tap,

tap,

tap!

Sid can tap.

31

# Book Bands for Guided Reading

The Institute of Education book banding system is a scale of colours that reflects the various levels of reading difficulty. The bands are assigned by taking into account the content, the language style, the layout and phonics. Word, phrase and sentence level work is also taken into consideration.

Maverick Early Readers are a bright, attractive range of books covering the pink to white bands. All of these books have been book banded for guided reading to the industry standard and edited by a leading educational consultant.

To view the whole Maverick Readers scheme, visit our website at

www.maverickearlyreaders.com

Or scan the QR code above to view our scheme instantly!